Here, There, and All Over the Place

Quips, Quotes, and "Quosters"

JOHNNY REMICK

Balboa Press books may be ordered through booksellers or by contacting:

Balboa Press
A Division of Hay House
1663 Liberty Drive
Bloomington, IN 47403
www.balboapress.com
1 (877) 407-4847

ISBN: 978-1-9822-0149-4 (sc)
978-1-9822-0148-7 (e)

Print information available on the last page.

Balboa Press rev. date: 05/09/2018

BALBOA.
PRESS
A DIVISION OF HAY HOUSE

Dedication

I humbly dedicate this book to my parents; the late Reverend Dr. Oscar E. and Emma L. Remick, who gave me life and showed me how to live it, love it, embrace it, observe it, and share it.

Acknowledgements

For me, writing "acknowledgements" is perhaps the most difficult part of the book. Influences and support run wide and deep. On one hand I do not want to leave anyone out and on the other hand I do not want the list to supersede the length of the book. I believe, like most people, our parents, siblings, extended family, friends, and co-workers and employers have all had major influences on our life. From my early school days in Chautauqua, New York and my high school years in Fredonia, New York and Alma, Michigan, my teachers, schoolmates, classmates and neighbors most definitely have had an impact on me and the way I view life. Professors, fellow students and "Phi Kappa Sigma" fraternity brothers at Adrian College, MI. have also had an impact on me, as well as my fellow stand-up comic buddies, and people I happen to meet on any given day. I am grateful for all of you, and all of it. I Thank You for all you add and have added to my life.

The following is a list of some of these amazing people whom I would like to affectionately acknowledge for varying contributions to the book:

Emma and Oscar Remick, Mark S. Remick, Paul T. Remick, Nancy Hunt-Remick, Nadine Alessi, Mary Avery, Anna Campbell, William "WillC" Clifton, Deborah Corday, Francesca Daniels, Alisa Davis, Susan Dietz, Kristy Eisenberg, Kurt Faust, Scott R. Harrison, Lora Harold, Mary Kushion, Bonnie and Fred Liener, Robert Mack, Sandy Merchant, Scott R. Miller, Rosemary Radisch, Kevin and Nancy Regan, Kent Roth, Brogan Schroeder, Susan Schroeder, Machelle Simpson, Sandy Watson.

Foreword

When Johnny "JR" Remick asked me to write the foreword for *Here, There, and All Over the Place*, I was at once honored and a little frustrated by the challenge of it all. Owing to our forty-year friendship, I quickly skipped over the honor part and dove right into the inevitable writer's block. I wasn't sure how to characterize Johnny so you, good reader, could appreciate him as I do. In Hollywood terms he would be a hyphenate, as in writer-actor-standup comic-webmaster-pop culture philosopher. In personal terms, he is a friend, confidante, officious intermeddler, surrogate brother, and the man who reunited me with Sandy Merchant, the love of my life. Put all those descriptors in your mental blender and out comes Johnny like one of those peanut butter shakes from Sonic . . . what ain't cool or smooth is just nuts. And I mean that in the best possible sense.

Here, There, and All Over the Place may be analogized best as if Mad Magazine had published Randy Pausch's *The Last Lecture*. This book captures Johnny's long-held, unique perspective on the interconnectedness we all share. You may find his sound-bite philosophies funny, irreverent, or poignant, but wherever they fall on your emotional spectrum they likely will make you rethink your view of life. *Here, There, and All Over the Place* simply, but pointedly, reminds us that we don't live life only for ourselves or by ourselves. No man is an island . . . except for Gilligan.

On a personal note, Sandy and I were there at the launch of Johnny's Facebook page **Make a Right Turn for Peace**. At the time it seemed a little incongruous with the JR whose most profound observation to date was the abrasive effect of Captain Crunch cereal on the roof of your mouth. These pages of quips, quotes, and "quosters", many of which first appeared on his **MARTFP** FB page, reflect the refinement of that mind. *I love you, man. No really, I do. This time I mean it.* –Enjoy!

Scott R. Harrison
Valparaiso Indiana

Table of Contents

Dedication iii

Acknowledgements iv

Foreword v

    I. Quosters 1

    II. Chalk Dust Philosophy 23

    III. simply said 29

    IV. Plainly Presented 37

About the Author 41

I. Quosters

a complimentary balance

of images and words

quote + poster = quoster

Time is never a barrier
between true friends
but a bridge of memories
that connects the soul,
as the river of familiarity
runs oh-so very deep.

LIFE
Live Love Laugh Learn
"L" YEAH!

It's pretty special when
someone's kind words
of appreciation mean so
much that our own mere
words cannot express it.

To effectively
communicate
we need to articulate...
People may not <u>like</u>
what we are saying, but
they first need to <u>know</u>
what we are saying, to
draw that conclusion.

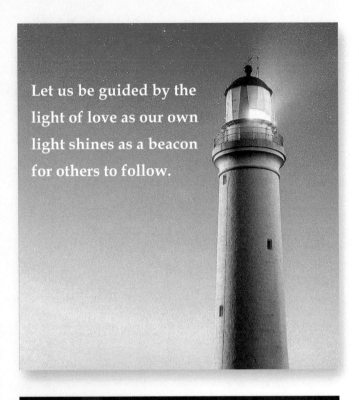

Let us be guided by the light of love as our own light shines as a beacon for others to follow.

Our actions speak more clearly of our good deeds than we could ever say. So, there is never really ever a need to recite that resume.

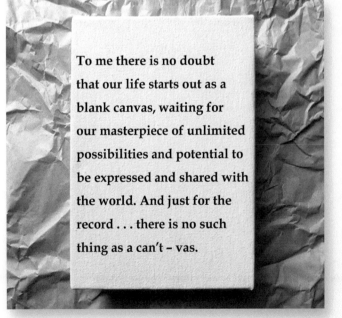

May the dance you dance take you wherever your heart and feet desire, as you dismiss the disrespect of the naysayers who lack the courage to even try to dance.

To me there is no doubt that our life starts out as a blank canvas, waiting for our masterpiece of unlimited possibilities and potential to be expressed and shared with the world. And just for the record . . . there is no such thing as a can't – vas.

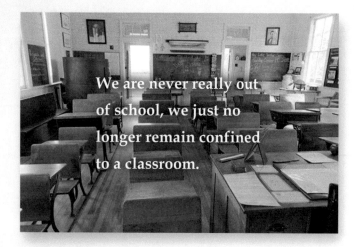

We are never really out of school, we just no longer remain confined to a classroom.

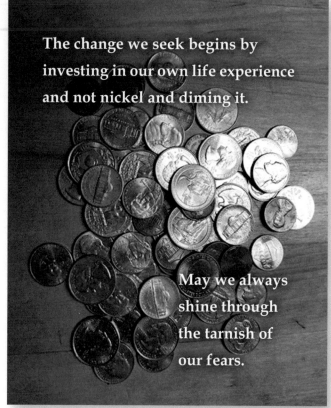

The change we seek begins by investing in our own life experience and not nickel and diming it.

May we always shine through the tarnish of our fears.

A compliment is an instrument that orchestrates harmony.

Blessings are blessings, whether we acknowledge them or not. In fact, for many of us the number is countless. But it is pretty amazing when we do stop to acknowledge and at least try to count them.

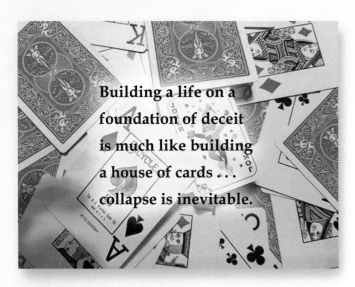

Building a life on a foundation of deceit is much like building a house of cards . . . collapse is inevitable.

I shall neither blame nor denounce myself for who I am not but, rather, acknowledge and embrace myself for who I am.

When I decide, Do-Or-Die . . . I have determined to be determined.

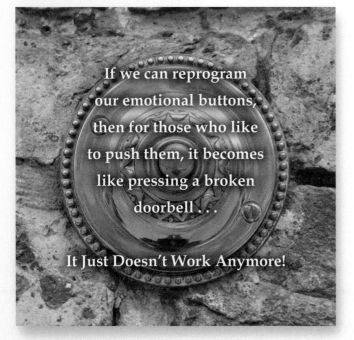

If we can reprogram our emotional buttons, then for those who like to push them, it becomes like pressing a broken doorbell . . .

It Just Doesn't Work Anymore!

Like the constant ebb and flow of the ocean, life comes and goes, brings us highs and lows and waits for absolutely no one.
It is of nature's secrets that we know not how . . .
the current of tide is timeless, the current of time is now.

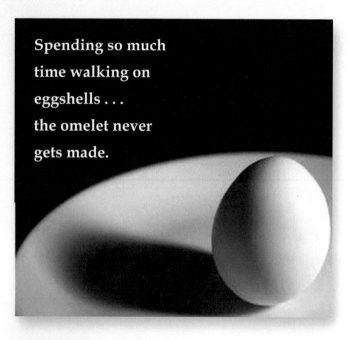

Spending so much
time walking on
eggshells . . .
the omelet never
gets made.

When we feed and cultivate
our seedlings of positive
and encouraging thought,
they develop into trees and
eventually forests of
unlimited possibilities.

Genuine Generosity has no Agenda

It is our grace and
not always the race
that gets us to where
we need to go.

You can be deep, sometimes steep
and at times rather shallow.
Things do get rocky with you and
you can be somewhat hollow.
In the grand scheme of things, you are
indescribable but you echo what I say.
My feelings for you are vast, like you Mr. Canyon . . .
HAVE A GREAT DAY . . . DAY Day day

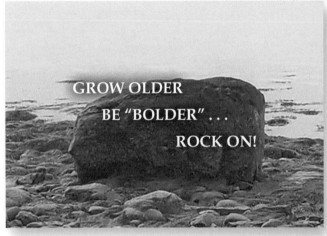

GROW OLDER
      BE "BOLDER" . . .
           ROCK ON!

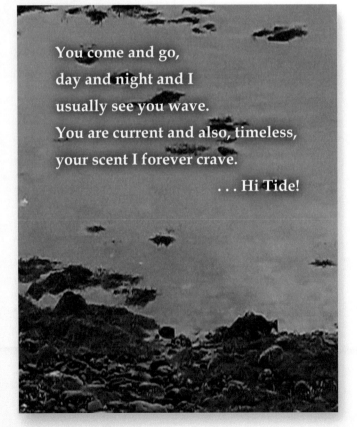

You come and go,
day and night and I
usually see you wave.
You are current and also, timeless,
your scent I forever crave.
         . . . Hi Tide!

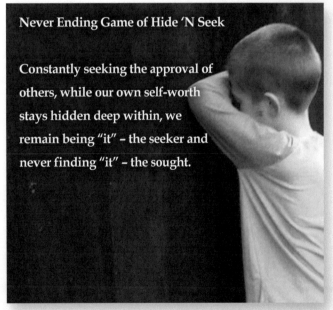

Never Ending Game of Hide 'N Seek

Constantly seeking the approval of
others, while our own self-worth
stays hidden deep within, we
remain being "it" – the seeker and
never finding "it" – the sought.

Don't Wait
To Take
A Leap
Of Faith . . .
HOP TO IT!

An answer to the seemingly rhetorical question, "What's the matter with the world today?" It is our tendency to forget that all lives matter in this world. . . every day.

The internet has caused the world to get so much smaller. But never as small as those who choose it, to use it, to hurt others.

I want people to cry
For only a moment when I die
Smile a long while because I was here
Laugh often for something I said or did
I know through these memories
I never really die
I will be here still
And through laughter
On and on I live

There are times we "live for"
the often-elusive moment;
striving for recognition,
accolades and fanfare.
Other times, we "live in"
the moment. . . just being.

No matter how heavy or how dark our world may get, let us be the ones who choose to keep it light. . . keep it lit.

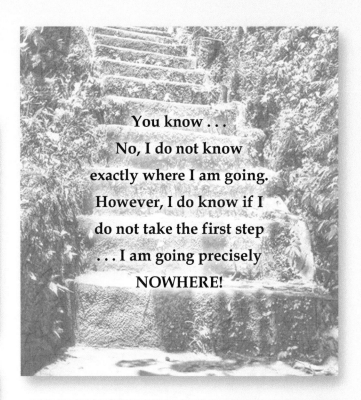

You know . . .
No, I do not know exactly where I am going. However, I do know if I do not take the first step . . . I am going precisely NOWHERE!

Laughter is indeed the best medicine, and I subscribe to that prescription.

Laughter IS the Best Medicine: we need not get a shot nor ingest and digest hills of pills, and we only have to "bend over. . ." because we hurt from laughing.

Well, you know it's a really busy day when you have a laundry list of things to do . . . and doing laundry isn't even on the list.

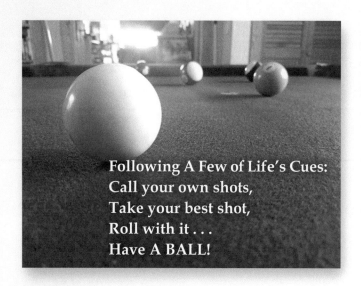

Following A Few of Life's Cues:
Call your own shots,
Take your best shot,
Roll with it . . .
Have A BALL!

Our light shines brightly
sometimes and at other times it
dims. there are often times
when our light flickers
and occasionally may even
go out . . . but never for too long.

LISTEN
SILENT
Two words, dependent on the same
letters and on each other... to exist.

In life, unlike in tennis . . .
LOVE IS EVERYTHING!

Love of self is the foundation for being able to truly love others and honestly accepting love from others.

The true majestic hue of love, liberty and democracy will always shine through the bogus and tragic darkness of hatred terrorism and tyranny.

The broken heart from the grief we feel after the death of a loved one, eventually returns to us as a treasure chest of memories that lives buried deep within us forever.

"Misery or Mystery"

We can accept the misery . . . a life of singing the blues so pitiful and tragic. Or we can embrace the mystery of life bringing us clues . . . so beautiful and magic.

The Heart:
Hears
Embraces
Attracts
Remembers
Trusts

The heart is deaf and reads no lips. how the heart hears . . . there are no words

Be it a shoulder to lean on, arms to lift up, a back to carry or a hand to lend . . . it is the heart we use to guide us with all of it.

The tempo to the soundtrack of our existence is kept by our own heartbeat.

You awaken from your slumber at the end of the night, only to be good and to keep things light. You brighten the day just at your sight, as I thank you and welcome you, morning.

Rare is that teacher we had in school for only a year and for whom we spend a lifetime being oh-so grateful. THANK YOU, MRS. AVERY! (3rd grade)

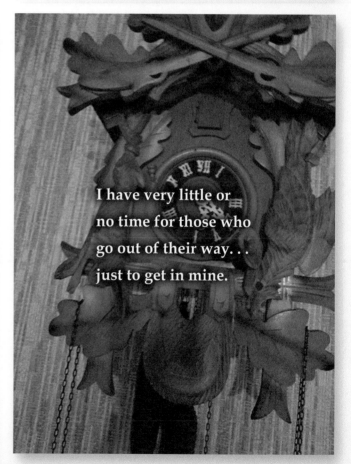

I have very little or no time for those who go out of their way. . . just to get in mine.

Opinionated debate can always wait . . . compassionate support cannot.

As we evolve, it is through conscious thought and action that we become directly involved with the direction of our own evolution

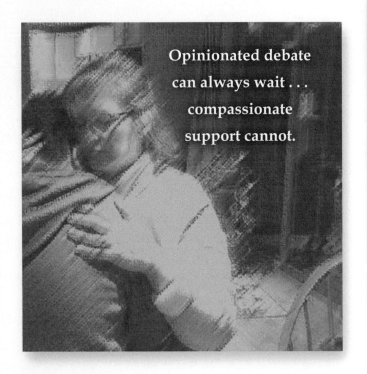

When we paint a picture of others . . . we also illustrate our own true colors.

Yep, I am going to have to start charging more than just a penny for my thoughts. Hmm, what was I think'n? . . . $20 Please!

WE CAN'T FAST FORWARD
TO THE FUTURE.
WE CAN'T REWIND
THE PAST.
LET'S PRESS PLAY...
LIVE TODAY!

A rainbow is rain's namesake
but equally it is the sun that makes
this colorful ribbon in the sky
something way beyond just color
that fills our eye

We share our true colors
through a rainbow of love,
compassion, kindness
and understanding.

Life, like a rainbow is colorful and
wonderful . . . so full of color and
oh-so full of wonder, and we
experience both, with and without
lightning and thunder.

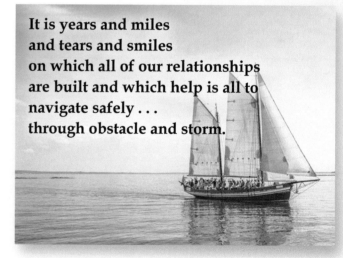

Our pursuit of excellence will always
include mistakes, blunders, goofs, gaffes,
errors, boo-boos, faux pas, uh-oh's and
. . . that is perfect!

It is years and miles
and tears and smiles
on which all of our relationships
are built and which help is all to
navigate safely . . .
through obstacle and storm.

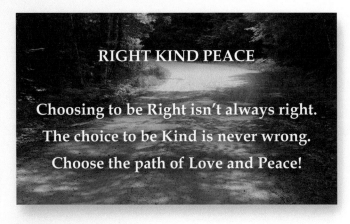

RIGHT KIND PEACE

Choosing to be Right isn't always right.
The choice to be Kind is never wrong.
Choose the path of Love and Peace!

Even if life tells us 'no', we can still always make a turn and change the direction of our own life at any time and find our own peace.

Respecting the journey of others, brings us all a bit closer home.

Yes, our five senses help to make up life's magic. But to lose our sense of humor, sense of self and sense of wonder . . . would be way more than tragic.

The sweet yet unheard serenade
of two distant hearts singing in unison –
a foreign, though somehow familiar tune.
The "forces of pull" so powerful –
beyond that of the fullest moon.
These unseen and unforeseen
forces reveal themselves –
that "this is meant to be."
Through un-seemingly connected events
the connection IS made . . . SERENDIPITY!

Two Rrrreally cool
things about
"A Smile" . . .

We SHARE IT!
while WE WEAR IT!

Who should really care if we choose
or dare to cheat at solitaire?
None, maybe one, after all this is
just harmless fun . . .
It just depends how you feel with it.
But cheating in real life cuts like a
knife and causes much strife . . .
there are so many others
that have to deal with it.

Throughout our lives
we can make strides
to step it up . . .
thus, preventing others
from stepping on, and
walking all over us.

When we keep "sweeping things under the rug" . . . someone is eventually going to trip and fall over the mounding hazard.

If we can be neither sympathetic nor empathetic, then that's just pathetic.

TEACH PEACE
LEARN TO LOVE
FIND FORGIVENESS

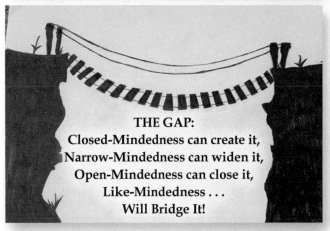

THE GAP:
Closed-Mindedness can create it,
Narrow-Mindedness can widen it,
Open-Mindedness can close it,
Like-Mindedness . . .
Will Bridge It!

To ever preserve our being
we need never limit our love,
reserve our resentment,
nor ration our compassion.

With whom I can
be completely
open, honest,
vulnerable and
raw, how is it you
can leave me . . .
in such total awe?

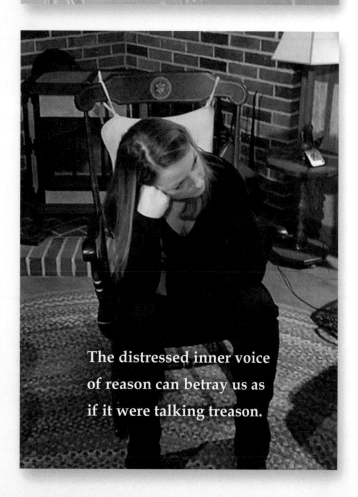

The distressed inner voice
of reason can betray us as
if it were talking treason.

Trust 'n Time

Trust can take *years* to build and *seconds* to break, however, it is through the *timeless* works of love and forgiveness that trust has the chance to be repaired and restored.

We have it within us . . .
to collectively cause a
tsunami of love, tolerance,
patience and understanding, thus
creating a calming ocean of peace
throughout this planet . . .
and BEYOND!

Our slow and steady
perseverance significantly
reduces our risk of falling
through the cracks of discontent.

Two
Fingers
One
Word
One
World!

Dressed in education,
armed with knowledge,
shielded by awareness,
allied with wisdom and
forever draped in love . . .
together we stand protected
against the tyranny
of ignorance.

IGNORANCE

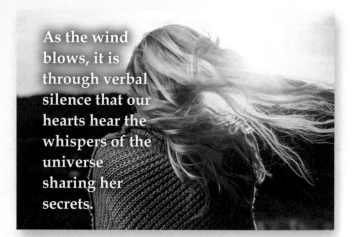

As the wind blows, it is through verbal silence that our hearts hear the whispers of the universe sharing her secrets.

Just because someone's point of view may differ from yours, it doesn't mean their vision isn't clear . . .

may yours and my vision remain very clear though some of our views may clearly vary

The gift of knowing I have done the right thing; an award that won't tarnish and is void of ever fading.

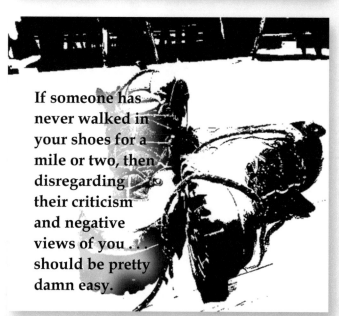

If someone has never walked in your shoes for a mile or two, then disregarding their criticism and negative views of you . . . should be pretty damn easy.

May we bring sunshine wherever we go and still have the grace to offer an umbrella to help others ward off rain.

We need not to be afraid <u>of change</u>, but aware of it. This awareness gives us the ability <u>to change</u> our fear to acceptance.

Limited time and unlimited love
Are what our fondest memories
are made of . . .

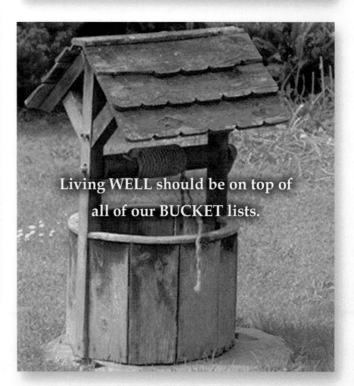

Living WELL should be on top of all of our BUCKET lists.

So, if opportunity for a better life is considered "greener pastures", then I think we could deem an envious rookie preacher . . . "a really green pastor".

As I age,
I discover
more and
more that
spending
time with
my friends. . .
never gets old.

By accepting to see life beyond my own distorted prism, I am refusing to remain stuck in a prison of my own delusion.

II. Chalk Dust Philosophy

thought-provoking and sometimes silly
thoughts presented on a chalkboard
. . . school is back in session

A Few Things About Me and Maybe You

I am very fond of "love",
anger makes me "mad"
and I truly detest "hate".
I am afraid of "fear" and
unsure about "uncertainty".
I am bummed at "sad"
and cheerful with "happy".
I am hopeful about "optimism"
and I have no concern about,
(you guessed it) . . . "apathy".

Big Cheese

Being the "Big Cheese" can be
rather difficult . . . particularly
if one is lactose intolerant.

Bounty

I believe putting a "Bounty"
on a self-absorbed person
would be rather redundant.

Fowl and Afraid

Being fearful of abruptly
quitting a bad habit, makes
one a cold – turkey chicken.

KEEP THE FAITH,
or. . . GET SOME!

GR FACTOR
THINGS LOOKING GRIM?
JUST BREATHE AND GRIN.
DON'T LOSE YOUR GRIP,
SHOW YOUR TRUE GRIT!

Grief and Faith

We cry when they die and we
grieve after they leave.
We try to cope and comprehend,
though we never forget.
It is more than just hope we will
see our loved ones again but also
our faith, that makes us so fortunate.

Hard to Believe

It's far easier for me to believe in
Santa Claus and The Easter Bunny
than it is for me to believe McDonald's®
will ever have a dollar menu at the
airport . . . or there will be
an express lane at Costco®

We Humans are Quite an Athletic Bunch . . .

We run late, we *skip* meals, we *hop* in the shower.
We *catch* a ride, we *hit* the road, we *fight* traffic,
we *pass* the time and we *punch* a clock. We have
been known to *jump* to conclusions, *push* the envelope
and *kick* the tires, yet also *step* back and *stand*
corrected. At the same time, we also *pull* for
the underdog, *throw* caution to the wind, *shoot* for
the stars and *lift* the spirits of those who need it.

<u>In the Meantime . . .</u>

While we are apart from the
ones we love, the meantime
can be a very mean time.

When we hit bottom,
it's time to kick butt!

To ponder death is not
to be morbid . . .
but rather, to be mortal.

Me, a Nudist?

Ironically, being a nudist
doesn't quite suit me . . .
nor anyone else, if you
actually, think about it.

Rock or Rocket?

With reluctance to learn,
we remain grounded.
With determination to learn,
the sky is the limit.

Selfish or Selfless?

Simply put; our selfishness
is a character flaw and
our selflessness . . .
a flawless characteristic.

When shadow boxing,
contact isn't necessary
. . . ever

Temper

We temper glass and steel to strengthen the piece. Adversely, our own temper can shatter, steal and weaken the peace.

Two Questions

Two questions that can never be answered honestly with "yes": Are you sleeping? Are you Dead?

WTF?
WIN THE FIGHT!

Conquering Life's Challenges with Bold Defiance

We need not stink up today with yesterday's crap.

III. simply said

a series of simple quotes and phrases
presented without all the confusion of
punctuation or capitalization
. . . pretty ordinarily stated

i am not really an ass
i am just kind of anal

so articulate is our intuition
when we just choose to listen

to be better instead of bitter
makes life so much sweeter

happiness is a lot like a butterfly
sometimes you just
have to wing it

capitalism is a great solution
but greed is a major problem

take a certain stance
make a circumstance

sometimes the circle of life
just makes me plain dizzy

we pay for our education but
class itself cannot be bought

compliments can lead
to confidence
and strengthen what
was once weak

yes i can be rather defiant to
the degree that if you agree
with me i may have to argue

sometimes i like to hear
an empathetic voice
other times i need to be
the sympathetic ear

victorious in faith
not a victim of fate

faith casts its shadow over doubt

may we forget about regret
and embrace the experience

forgiving is not about forgetting
it is about remembering to heal

good health is the
greatest of wealth

the planted seed of grace
and gratitude flourishes

let us be grateful for all
the good we have
and not hateful for the
goods others have

the spirit moves us
our body grooves us
the vibe behooves us

plant a smile and reap
a happy harvest

keep moving forward
the healing will follow

i would not say that
i am immature

i am just prolonging
my adolescence

we cannot be arrested
for what we think

but our negative thoughts
do imprison us

i believe that life is
a state of mind

and we choose the zip
code to reside

without true forgiveness
we honestly forgo peace

we give a piece of ourselves by
sharing our peace with others

we are poised to love or
we are poisoned by fear

just one good reason
to do something
transcends a hundred
excuses not to

the receipt we receive for
our deceit is disharmony

we cannot relive
but we can forgive

we all possess the license
to renew our

dreams at any time and
it never expires

this sounds kind of crazy but

being a bit nuts keeps us sane

we all have a few screws loose

many of us just mute the rattle

thought is the very
thing that counts

for our thoughts account
for everything

that seemingly unconditional
relationship

then all of a sudden here
comes a condition

yesterday is unlike underwear

because you cannot change it

the most down to earth people
are usually the most uplifting

for all of our numerous
uh oh moments

we also have our beautiful
aha moments

IV. Plainly Presented

a small sample of quips and some deeper
thoughts presented in a homespun manner
. . . it's all here in black and white

Oh, the Irony . . .
That precious millennial, who believes
that "giving 110%" is virtually impossible
. . . after graduating with a 4.5 grade point.

The parallel is not too farfetched;
thus, way from being wild –
it takes one to dream and many to make
a dream come true. . . as the proverb,
'It takes a village to raise a child.'

The apology that was
sincerely asked for and
genuinely accepted yesterday,
should never, ever, have to be
defended today.

The best teachers are the ones
who are most in tune, whether
they teach us music or whether
they guide us in some other way.

Compassion carries
immeasurable weight,
while Callousness bears
unbounded burden.

"We have dominion over our opinion."
. . . this simply means we have
profound control over when,
where, why, or whether to express it.

May we never squelch
the dreams of a dreamer,
for dreams keep the
nightmares away.

It is my enlightenment through
age and wisdom that I find,
it is my body getting older
that has changed my mind.

The Fashion of Compassion . . .

It is not something we wear, it
is something we share, and it
never goes out of style.

When the 5th commandment says,
"Honor thy *Father* and thy *Mother*",
I believe it has as much to do with
respecting *Time* and *Nature*
as it does our parents.

"Physical" and "Fiscal"

We can learn a lot from
those who come from very
little, and who appreciate the
little things oh-so very much.

You know, in addition to fiscal responsibility when
it comes to my own healthcare, it also makes a lot of
sense to me (and for me) to be a bit more physically
responsible in caring for my own individual health.

In regard to beer, the word pound
is a verb and is also a noun.
In this "case" I know from
personal experience that when I
simply *verb* a great deal, then
I certainly gain a lot of plural *noun*.

Simple, quiet,
calm moments
of just breathing
the same air
. . . few words
even spoken.

Bigger than the
biggest fanfare,
with silence
barely broken.

To me, sense of self and sense of
humor . . . one in the same.

Success is not the measure
of 'lots of stuff' . . .
but the treasure of knowing
and accepting what
you got is enough.

We can catch it or we can miss it,
we can accept it or dismiss it, when
"reading the writing on the wall", is the case.

Though, when we choose not to read it or
just plain don't see it, reality can be like
spray paint in the face.

About the Author

Johnny Remick, a Maine native, has literally lived coast to coast. . . and back again.

Living much of his life in Michigan, he graduated from Alma High School, earned a Bachelor of Arts degree (Theater) from Adrian College and continued onto Specs Howard School for Broadcast Arts, which all helped in launching a successful career as a voiceover artist, commercial actor and a national touring professional stand-up comedian/impressionist from Detroit.

He relocated several years later to Los Angeles in his continued pursuit of acting.

Johnny (along with his two brothers) were taught to embrace diversity and express individuality, while extending kindness, consideration, compassion and understanding to others and self, by their loving parents. Oscar and Emma Remick bestowed upon their three sons the significance of living a life of service and modeling it by their own service to church, to community and to numerous academic and world-wide communities.

Adding to Johnny's inherent sense of humor is his mindfulness of self, combined with a profound sense of compassion for others. He respects and appreciates the power of words and their ability to cut, heal, create laughter and tears, and ignite perspective/retrospective. Inevitably, he was drawn to create "Make a Right Turn for Peace" (www.facebook.com/makearightturnforpeace), a non-partisan, universal grassroots movement, sharing the message of love, peace, understanding, forgiveness with lightheartedness and humor.

For 18-years Johnny Remick made America laugh. Although he retired from the comedy stage in 2007, he continued commercial acting and material writing for his comedic peers. He moved back to his family home on the Maine Coast during the summer of 2017 to focus on writing.

WELCOME TO MY SHOP! Please check out (www.cafepress.com/coolstuffmartfp) where you can find many of Johnny's "quips, quotes and quosters" on t-shirts, mugs, stationary and other cool stuff.

Printed in the United States
By Bookmasters